ORCHIDS

ORCHIDS

PHOTOGRAPHS BY MANUEL AUBRON

TEXT BY PASCAL DESCOURVIÈRES

Contents

Preface

Orchids captivate me by the diversity of their shapes and textures, by their startling contrasts in color and species, and by their subtle, often intoxicating aroma.

I came upon my first orchids while hiking in the Queyras mountain range almost fifteen years ago. Fascinated by their beauty, by the strangeness of their flowers, and, scientifically, by the unique strategies they employ to attract pollinating insects, I began to photograph them in their natural habitat. I trekked through the Himalayas, admiring a spectacular species of epiphyte tropical orchids, and subsequently began growing them in greenhouses. I traveled to South America, where I explored different, extremely rich biological milieus such as the biotopes in the Andes and in humid jungles.

My photographs were taken to capture the elusive allure of these vibrant plants.

Manuel Aubron

Orchids have seduced not only amateur naturalists and botanists, but also a larger public, especially since hybrids have become frequently featured in garden centers. Cultivating these plants is now common, yet plenty of genera remain rare and difficult to maintain. In their natural environment, some species of orchids have already disappeared. Others are still present, but for how much longer? Their survival remains dependent upon a number of financial, economic, and ecological factors.

Certainly, it would be best to preserve these flowers in their natural environment. Yet they are rapidly disappearing, year after year, often victims of anarchic deforestation, of uncontrolled urban sprawl, or of changing climate laws. In metropolitan France, too many species are on the road to extinction. Sometimes, however, only small protective steps, such as mowing the greenery on the sides of the roads, are required to keep terrestrial orchids flowering and fructifying.

Most orchids require strict ecological conditions, which makes them vulnerable. That hundreds have disappeared should alert us of the increasing risk of a massive and irreversible extinction of species, like our planet experienced 65 million years ago after the impact of a meteorite. But let's leave the past behind…and act!

Pascal Descourvières

South America

Tropical South America possesses a rich variety of flora, largely because its climates are so diverse. Southern regions are temperate and have no epiphyte orchids, which live on trees. Instead, this region is known for its numerous terrestrial species, which are vividly colored and fragrant. The tropics can be subdivided into several zones with well-defined characteristics: the Amazonian basin, mostly situated in Brazil and the countries that border it, where low-altitude, relatively homogenous forests possess an impressive epiphyte flora; the Guyana plateau; and the Andes mountains and surrounding areas. The orchid diversity in these mountains is extraordinary, resulting from the immense richness of the different biotopes according to altitude, rainfall, cardinal direction, and geographic isolation, among other factors. Many species are unique to these regions; in particular, certain species of *Masdevallia* are incredibly rare and valuable, present only in one tiny valley, at a precise altitude.

Pleurothallist gargantuan as an epiphyte on a tree trunk, Ecuador

Bollea ecuadorana

The *Bollea* genus includes almost a dozen species scattered in the middle altitudes of the Andes mountains. Most of these grow in Colombia, which alone possesses nine species of *Bollea*—unsurprising, given that Colombia has one of the highest levels of biodiversity in the world.

Species of this genus lack pseudobulbs, but have long, ribbonlike leaves. The subtle bluish tinge of their flowers, so rare in the center of orchids, is exceptional. They can reach three to four inches in breadth.

Bollea pulvinaris

Catasetum ornithoides

Cataseum ornithoides is an original genus with unisexual flowers—a rare case among orchids. The same plant can produce either a flowering stem of male flowers, often quite decorative, or a flowering stem of female flowers, generally greenish and very similar from one species to another.

The flower shown here is male and, like all *Catasetum*, posesses an ingenious propulsion system that catapults pollen onto visiting insects.

Cattleya mendelii

The aristocrat of orchids, *Cattleya* were at the center of the 'orchid-mania' that ravaged Europe—particularly the United Kingdom—during the nineteenth century.

The *Cattleya mendellii* has a smaller bearing and carries two or three elegant flowers, which stretch six to eight inches across. *Cattleya* plants are often hybridized with others in their genus, as well as with neighboring genera. Over a hundred new hybrids are catalogued every month. *Cattleya leopoldi* is a large Brazilian orchid, which reaches a height of three feet, and can carry over ten heavy flowers, colored warm bronze and violet.

Cattleya leopoldii

Comparettia macroplectron

The *Comparettia* genus includes few species, but all are small plants with exceptionally vivid flowers. They possess a nectar-containing spur behind the labellum. The two species shown here come from middle-altitude regions of Colombia.

Comparettia macroplectron has very large flowers, stretching approximately two inches across, colored a pinkish-purple, while *Comparettia ignea* has brilliant orange flowers.

Comparettia ignea

Dracula vampira

The hanging flowers of this orchid resemble enigmatic masks, and have names that lend an added sense of mystery: *Dracula vampira* (vampire), *Dracula chiroptera* (bat), *Dracula chimaera* (chimera), *Dracula diabola* (devil).

Dracula vampira is one of the rarest and most prized representatives of this genus, whose approximately one hundred species come from mountainous regions of the Andes, particularly Colombia and Ecuador. They grow in forests at an elevation of 1,600 to 10,000 feet, and are continously enveloped in fog, which means that cultivation must occur in a cold and humid greenhouse. The shape of this flower is unusual: its three sepals are stuck together, each prolonged by a long filament, with very small petals that are difficult to discern.

Elleanthus discolor

Elleanthus is a genus of approximately 120 species found throughout tropical America, particularly in the Andes. These plants are most often terrestrial, and have tight groupings of long bamboo-like canes that are often taller than three feet in height. The flowers, small and discreet, are numerous and grouped together at the end of the stem, and are often brightly colored with red, orange, or pink tones, like the two shown here. They are pollinated by hummingbirds, who are attracted to their vivid colors and the shape of their tube. In *Elleanthus amethystinoides*, the green bracts are much longer than the length of the flowers.

Elleanthus amethystinoides

Gongora chocoensis

Gongoras are epiphytes with pseudobulbs pressed tightly together, each topped with one very veiny leaf. Some species live in symbiosis with ants that build their nests in the mass of the pseudobulbs, a condition which also exists with orchids such as the *Coryanthus*.

The vivid flowering stem emerges from the base of a mature pseudobulb and hangs below the plant. In certain species, like *Gongora chocoensis,* it can reach over three feet in length and bear tens of flowers that look like wild birds. In cultivation, these flowers are most often grown in hanging baskets.

Gongora ecornuta

Lepanthes lucifer

Lepanthes are miniature orchids that most often grow discreetly in the humid moss of the mountainous regions of Central America and the Andes. *Lepanthes lucifer,* a species endemic to humid Ecuatorian forests at altitudes off 4,000 to 5,000 feet, barely reaches an inch in height. Its vivid flower is garnished in the center with two small horns, which give the species its devilish name.

Also among the 947 species that make up this genus is *Lepanthes magnifica,* whose pretty flowers are relatively large for this genus (nearly half an inch), and contain flowering stems that rest on the leaf and produce flowers for several years in succession. Curiously, the other peduncles of this plant form a structure that resembles a fish bone.

Lepanthes magnifica

Masdevallia papillosa

In England during the 19th century, *Masdevallia* plants were largely cultivated by orchid amateurs because they prospered in lightly-heated greenhouses and blossomed abundantly. Today, this vast genus of nearly six hundred species has been somewhat forgotten, possibly because the plants have a reputation for being difficult to cultivate.

In reality, the majority of *Masdevallia* grow well in a temperate greenhouse. Many are miniatures with flowers almost bigger than the plant and with warm, gem-like colors, like the aptly-named *Masdevallia papillosa*, which blossoms in Ecuador at an altitude of approximately 6,500 feet. Much less common is *Masdevallia manoloi*, a species rarely seen in cultivation, which was discovered in the upper altitudes of Peru in 1997. Its dramatic flowers can reach eight inches in height.

Masdevallia manoloi

Maxillaria pulla

This vast genus includes approximately 700 species. The structure of the plant varies fairly dramatically from species to species, though the flowers are fairly uniform, with a triangular shape, free-standing petals and sepals, and a unifloral flowering stem.

Maxillaria pulla has subtle coloring, and grows in Colombia, Ecuador, Peru, and Bolivia, at altitudes of 7,000 to 9,000 feet. The Peruvian and Ecuadorian *Maxillaria sanderiana* is known for the size of its flowers, which can stretch six inches across. Its flowering stems grow on the substrate, sometimes rooting themselves before emerging to exhibit long-lasting flowers, whose colors range from white to crimson.

Maxillaria sanderiana

Miltoniopsis vexillaria
'Josefina'

Miltoniopsis are the parents of the hybrid often known as the "pansy orchid." This genus includes six graceful, pastel-toned species, which thrive in foggy mountain forests. Their labellum is large, flat, and fragile in appearance, with yellow tones at the base.

Miltoniopsis vexillaria has a wide geographic distribution: it can be found in Columbia at altitudes of 3,200 to 7,200 feet, as well as in Ecuador. *Miltoniopsis phalaenopsis* is a species endemic to Colombia, and can only be found in the region of Antioquia.

Miltoniopsis phalaenopsis

Oncidium eurycline

The genus *Oncidium* includes a multitude of species distributed over Central and South America, whose flowering stems often bear numerous yellow flowers marked with brown. *Oncidium eurycline* is a small plant with particularly luminous flowers, whose bright yellow labellum contrasts with the rest of the reddish-brown flower. This species can sometimes be cultivated in gardens, as it is in the Antilles, where the flowers are known charmingly as "golden bees."

Not every *Oncidium* flowers is yellow, however: the *Oncidium dayanum*, also known as *Caucaea dayana*, has more traditional white blooms, spotted with purple.

Oncidium dayanum

Paphinia rugosa
var. *kalbreyeri*

In the Cretan town of Paphos, *Paphinia* is one of the names given to the goddess Aphrodite. This orchid was thus named for its stunning flowers, which stretch nearly four inches across. Sadly, they typically last for only five days, though the plant produces several successive flowering stems, extending the blossoming time over a few months. The twelve species of this genus are found in tropical South America, on the lower side of mossy tree trunks and in the underbrush. In cultivation, they require reduced light and an elevated, constant humidity.

Paphinia rugosa is a charming, star-shaped Colombian species. *Paphinia herrerae* originates from Ecuador and produces a hanging stem, containing two to five large flowers ranging from pale pink to light red, which reach a breadth of nearly five inches.

Paphinia herrerae

Phragmipedium besseae

There are more than twenty species of *Phragmipedium,* which, aside from a few species of the *Selenipedium* genus, are the only lady's slippers in South America. The majority of *Phragmipediums* grow on mossy rocks and river beds, where their roots are sometimes immersed. Thankfully, replicating these conditions is not necessary for cultivation.

Phragmipeduim bessae, with its vividly colored red, orange, or yellow flowers, was first discovered in Peru. *Phragmipedium schlimii* grows in Colombia near Medellín and Ocaña on humid, eastern slopes, at altitudes ranging from 4,500 to 6,200 feet. It has small, pleasantly-scented pink flowers, which spread over a flowering stem that is approximately twelve inches long. *Phragmipeduim bessae* and *Phragmipedium schlimii* are often used in hybridization, resulting in flowers with beautiful colors and a compact bearing.

Phragmipedium schlimii

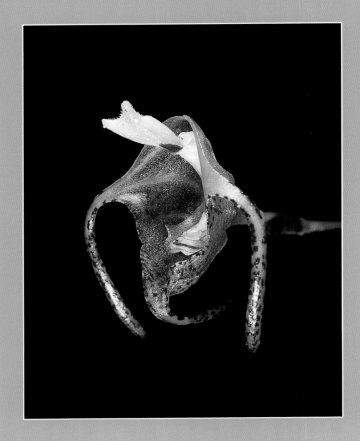

Porroglossum jesupiae

Porroglossum is a genus that encompasses thirty small species, similar to the *Masdevallia*. These species are distributed mostly in misty forests in Colombia and Venezuela, though they can also be found in Bolivia and Peru.

The flowering stem of the *Porroglossum* extends past the leaves and bears a strange flower whose three sepals, two lateral petals, and labellum are fairly difficult to distinguish. The latter, lodged at the center of the cup formed by the three sepals, is articulated and thus mobile. When a pollinating insect arrives, it lands on the labellum, which moves so that the insect's head bumps against a pollen deposit, or deposits other pollens on the sticky stigma, guaranteeing that the plant is pollinated and will reproduce.

Porroglossum dreisei

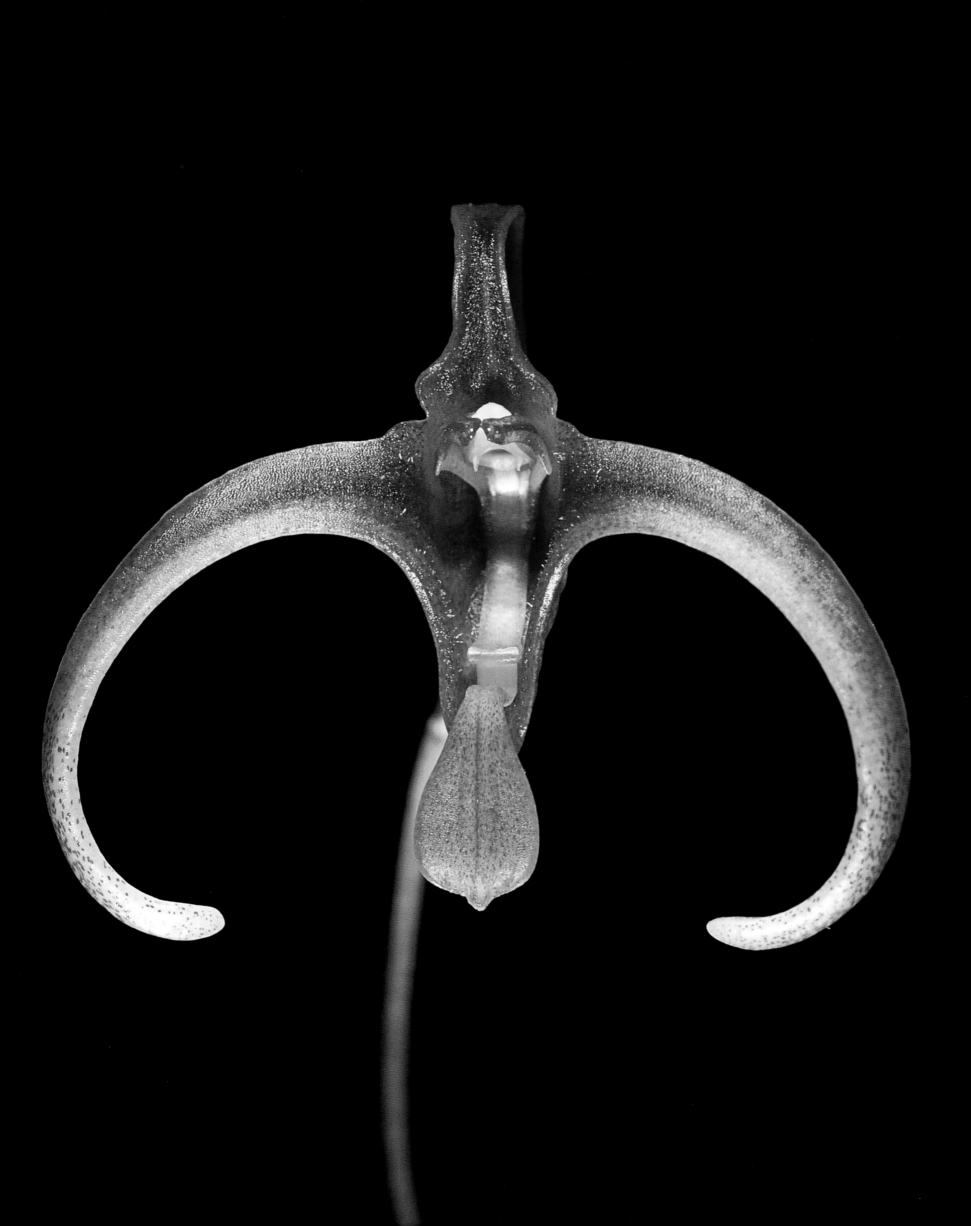

Prosthechea widgrenii

Recently, certain species from the *Encyclia* genus were regrouped into a new genus created especially for them: the *Prosthechea*. The creation of this genus was encouraged both by visible differences, and by the results of multiple DNA tests. Its purpose was partly to reorganize, and partly to clarify parental relations, as these species have numerous criteria that make them completely separate from *Encyclia*. Many of these criteria are anatomical: the labellum, for example, is atop the flower, instead of below as it is with most orchids.

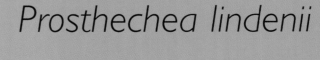

Prosthechea lindenii

Restrepia sanguinea

The *Restrepia* genus includes 51 species distributed between Mexico and Bolivia, the majority of which are found in Colombia. The plants form little tufts, each with several coarse leaves. Each leaf, nearly as wide as it is tall, is carried by a stem covered with bracts that dry out. The flowers of these plants are red, pink, or orange, and are born at the base of the leaf and carried by a thin, long peduncle.

This genus is unique for its two lower sepals, which are large and soldered together to form a vividly colored synsepal. The upper sepal is long and thickens at the tip, causing it to resemble an insect's antenna. *Restrepia sanguinea* and *chameleon* are two Colombian types.

Restrepia chameleon

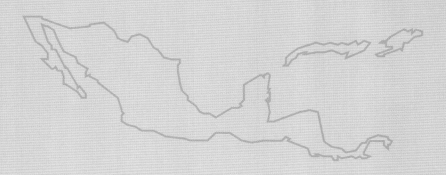

Central America

From southern Mexico to northern Colombia, Central America is characterized by rich, diverse climates distributed over a tiny territory, which makes it ideal for an explosion of species. Such diversity is due largely to mountainous regions with active volcanoes. Areas near the Caribbean are more humid than those near the Pacific Ocean, causing some regions to have a very dry season, while others remain constantly buried in fog.

Tropical forest surrounding a Mayan temple, Guatemala

Barkeria shoemakeri

This genus, similar to *Epidendrum,* contains sixteen species and is principally present in Mexico and Guatemala, though it can also be found in Costa Rica and Panama. The plants are shaped like canes, and bloom—often very plentifully—at one end.

Barkeria shoemakeri grows at an altitude of nearly 2,000 feet, near river banks in very dry zones. Outside of its natural environment, it must be cultivated on a support rather than in a pot. In the winter, these plants must also be given a resting period, during which they should receive little water and much light. *Barkeria lindleyana* has beautiful, large flowers that flourish over two to three months. The majority of the species live in tropical zones that benefit from a long, particularly dry season, during which the plants rest and lose part of their leaves. Certain species even live as epiphytes on cacti.

Barkeria lindleyana

Epidendrum gomezii

More than 1,100 species can be classified as *Epidendrum*. Some of these species are tiny, while others have giant cane-like stems that stretch over six feet long. They are widely distributed from Florida through Northern Argentina.

Epidendrum gomezii is a Mexican orchid. *Epidendrum criniferum*, which grows primarily in mountainous regions of Panama, is a medium-sized species with delicate flowers, whose labellum is lightly barbed.

Epidendrum criniferum

Galeandra dives

Galeandra dives is originally a Columbian species. Its plants have long, cylindrical pseudobulbs, garnished with markedly veiny leaves, which often fall in drier seasons. Their inflorescence is apical and boasts numerous flowers, each of whose horn-like labellum has a spine.

Galeandra greenwoodii is a recently discovered species that grows in Mexico. Its long-lasting flowers can bloom for up to three months, and are among the largest and most colorful of this genus, which includes 26 species distributed across tropical America.

Galeandra greenwoodii

Laelia anceps
'Guerrero'

The *Laelia* genus encompasses over sixty elegant, vividly colored species, distributed principally between Brazil and Central America. It is very similar to *Cattleya*, and horticulturalists have often tried to hybridize the two.

At the heart of the *Laelia* genus there is a group of species that originate in Mexico and Central America, which includes *Laelia anceps*. This is one of the most common Mexican species of this genus and is frequently spotted, although its appearance changes depending on the climate in which it grows. *Laeliea anceps semi alba*, for example, has flowers that are almost entirely white, while those in the Guerrero region have a yellowish labellum, and plants around the Gulf of Mexico have pink blossoms.

Laelia anceps semi alba

Lycaste bradeorum

There are 22 species of *Lycaste*, distributed principally in Central America. Named for one of the most beautiful women of Antiquity, the sister of Helen of Troy, *Lycaste* are similar to the genera *Ida* and *Anguloa*, and possess a profusion of brightly-colored, triangular flowers. The genus includes approximately fifteen species that lose their leaves during the drier season, and whose leafless pseudobulbs are armed with several sharp thorns.

Lycaste bradeorum, a medium-sized plant, blooms prodigiously in the springtime, and has aromatic flowers that are approximately two inches wide. *Lycaste deppei*, which is widely disseminated in central America, grows as an epiphyte in humid, mountainous tropical forests. Its bold flowers measure approximately three inches wide.

Lycaste deppei

Maxillaria tenuifolia

Maxillaria tenuifolia grows rapidly, forming great tufts of pseudobulbs topped by a long, narrow, arched leaf. In the springtime, the dark red flowers bloom in profusion and exhale a captivating coconut scent.

Maxillaria praestans comes from Mexico and Guatemala and possesses hearty, elegant flowers, approximately two to four inches high, whose dark, tongue-shaped labellum contrasts sharply with the five brightly colored parts of the flower.

Maxillaria praestans

Polycycnis barbata

This species inhabits the mountainous, humid regions of Costa Rica and Panama, producing long-flowering stems, either hanging or arched, along with large, beautifully-colored flowers. The tiny labellum is less than an inch long, and is festooned with bizarre little barbs. The column or gynostemium, however, is long and curved, like the neck of a swan, after whom this genus is named—*polycycnis* translates directly as "many swans."

Psychopsis krameriana

These 'butterfly orchids' belong to a small genus of tropical American epiphytes, similar to the *Oncidium*. The flat, tight pseudobulbs, each with a thick leaf spotted in brown and red, are almost melded to the substrate. The flowering stem is exceptionally long, and often measures more than three feet. It boasts large flowers that develop successively over several years, so that an adult plant is always in bloom.

The four species of *Psychopsis* differ in such tiny details that they are often difficult to distinguish from one another. *Psychopsis krameriana* can be differentiated from more common species such as *Psychopsis papilio* by the end of its flowering stem, which is rounded, rather than flat. It exists primarily in Panama and Costa Rica, but also in South America, west of the Andes, at sea level through altitudes of up to 3,300 feet.

Rhynchostele maculata

The genus *Rynchostele*, also known under the name *Lemboglossum*, groups together several species present only in Central America, from Mexico to Costa Rica. These species require relatively cool temperatures for cultivation.

Rhynchostele maculata, whose long flowering stems can be up to two feet high, grows as an epiphyte in Guatemala and Mexico, at altitudes of 6,500 and 10,000 feet. It boasts several large flowers, each approximately two inches wide. *Rhyncostele cervantesii*, a small plant with large flowers that stretch from one to three inches, grows in Mexico, either as an epiphyte on pine and oak trees, or on rocks, always at altitudes of 4,500 to 10,500 feet.

Rhynchostele cervantesii

Rossioglossum insleayi

Rossioglossum, a genus similar to *Odontoglossum*, includes six species native to the region between Mexico and Panama. *Rossioglossum insleayi* is a Mexican plant whose flowers, nearly three inches wide, are brightly speckled and aromatic. In cultivation, these species require cool climates in order to prosper.

Rossioglossum grande is known primarily for the size of its flowers, which are over six inches wide. Although the plant is fairly compact, each mature pseudobulb produces one to two flowering stems that possess two to eight flowers apiece, and are approximately a foot in length.

Rossioglossum grande

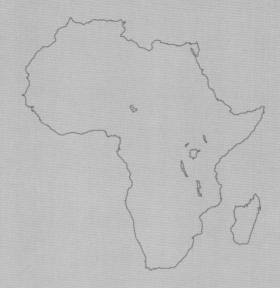

Africa

North Africa boasts terrestrial orchids very similar to those found in Mediterranean Europe. Regions south of the Sahara possess a variety of orchid families, particularly in the mountains and in tropical forests. The majority of the species have white flowers marked with green or pink, often with a long, nectar-giving spike. Malawi, a small state whose altitude reaches nearly 10,000 feet, has the richest orchid flora in tropical Africa, due largely to the almost Mediterranean climate, which fosters a vibrant endemic flora. The geographically-isolated island of Madagascar is also an orchid haven, with many exclusive native species.

Aerial view of an equatorial forest and its canopy, Cameroon.

Aerangis fastuosa

Aerangis includes sixty or so species, half of which are found in humid regions of tropical Africa, the other half of which are native to Madagascar and its surrounding islands. (One lone species, curiously, is instead native to Sri Lanka). These monopodial orchids possess long, nectar-filled spurs, and usually bear hanging flowering stems of white flowers, often marked with green or salmon pink. At sundown, many species give off a strong perfume redolent of narcissus or hyacinth, which attracts nocturnal butterflies who come to collect the nectar and pollinate the flower.

Aerangis fastuosa is present in Madagascar's perennially green, humid forests situated at altitude levels of 3,000 to 5,000 feet. *Aerangis decaryana* is an epiphyte plant that grows in the drier regions of the island.

Aerangis decaryana

Aeranthes ramosa

Aeranthes is a small genus comprised of approximately thirty species distributed throughout Africa, primarily in Madagascar and its neighboring islands. Its unique beauty makes it a popular plant for cultivation. *Aeranthes ramosa* has slender, hanging flowering stems, three to seven feet long, each with multiple translucent green blossoms. In cultivation, these species require shade and elevated platforms, so that their stems can hang properly.

Aeranthes henrici is a medium-sized plant with beautiful dark green leaves, thick roots, and a relatively short flowering stem. It has several white flowers, each with a green labellum, that stretch up to eight feet wide.

Aeranthes henrici

Ancistrochilus rothschildianus

The name *Ancistrochilus* comes from the Greek term for "spiked lips" (ankistron cheilos), and was given to this orchid because of the hooked shape of the labellum's middle lobe. These epiphyte plants are distributed throughout western Africa, and possess small, conical pseudobulbs, topped with thin, wrinkled leaves which fall in the drier season, just before flowering. Usually quite discreet, this species then exhibits gorgeous flowers that stretch approximately two inches wide, and are pink, purple, or white with a bright purple labellum.

Angraecum eichlerianum

These two orchids belong to a vast genus of 200 species, and is similar to *Aerangis*. *Angraecum* includes species both miniature and giant, some with tiny green blossoms, others with large, fragrant white flowers tinted green or pink. The climate for these plants varies: some require full sun; others need the shade of humid forests, as is the case for *Angraecum germinyanum*, which grows east of Madagascar and in the Comoro Islands.

Angraecum eichlerianum possesses a long stem that can reach over sixteen feet in length, allowing it to stretch between the trees and find its way toward light. This species has delicate flowers, approximately four inches wide, and lives in Angola, Cameroon, Gabon, Nigeria, and Zaire.

Angraecum germinyanum

Ansellia africana

Ansellia Africana spreads expansively throughout tropical Africa, from the Ivory Coast to Kenya, and differs slightly in color and structure from region to region. It is a large plant that often lives as an epiphyte on thick tree branches in well-lit locations. Its pseudobulbs, robust and squeezed tightly together, can reach one to four feet in height, depending on the variety. After a significant resting period, the plants become entirely covered with flowers, which are two inches across, headily fragrant, and differ slightly in color from one species to the next, though the standard coloring is pure yellow or yellow spotted with brown.

Bulbophyllum barbigerum

The genus *Bulbophyllum* is extraordinarily diverse, with over 1,800 species present principally in Asia and Australia. It is characterized by pseudobulbs that are generally spherical, each topped with a single leaf. Each flower has a moving labellum, which gives the plant the appearance of crawling.

In general, the seventy species found in Africa have quietly-colored flowers. *Bulbophyllum barbigerum* is common throughout western Africa. An epiphyte that grows in humid forests, it is always found in the shade, at low to medium altitudes. Its flowers, approximately one inch wide, are clustered together, and have striking labella covered in reddish-brown hairs. Its sister species, *Bulbophyllum vulcanicum,* is from the mountainous zones of Malawi, Zaire, Uganda, Rwanda, and Burundi.

Bulbophyllum vulcanicum

Cymbidiella rhodochila
(in bud)

The three species of this genus are endemic to Madagascar. Their bearing is similar to that of *Cymbidium,* though overall they have more in common with *Eulophiella. Cymbidiella rhodochila,* also known as *Cymbidiella pardalina,* grows as an epiphyte atop the large fern *Platycerium madagascariensis.* Its robust bloom stretches three feet tall, and carries large, long-lasting flowers, known for their bright red labella.

Cymbidiella rhodochila

Tridactyle bicaudata

Tridactyle bicaudata is found as an epiphyte or a lithophyte throughout tropical Africa, from Ethiopia to South Africa, and from the Ivory Coast to Malai. Its inflorescences carry eight to twenty heavily perfumed flowers, displayed in two rows that bloom simultaneously. At the center of the labellum is an opening, which allows the pollinating insect to access the nectar in the spur.

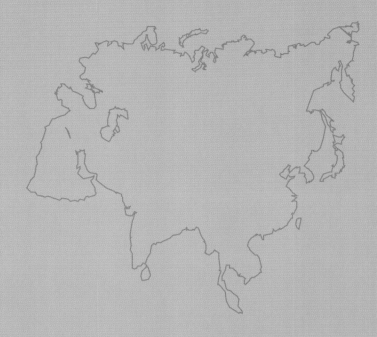

Asia

Asian flora is rich, varied, and expansive. The island of Borneo, with its hot and humid climate, is an ideal environment for orchids: the slopes of Mount Kinabalu alone host almost seven hundred species. Other climates demand a heartier character. Orchids native to the many regions that experience monsoons have adapted to sharp weather contrasts—as is the case for the numerous deciduous *Dendrobium*—while Himalayan orchids can famously survive frost. Among these diverse genera, some are endemic only to Asia, including the rare *Paphiopedilum*.

Tree with numerous epiphytes, including **Dendrobium**, Nepal.

Bulbophyllum sumatranum

Bulbophyllum have exceptional flowers, particularly those in southeast Asia and in certain surrounding islands. Sometimes considered to be a variant of the Sumatran *Bulbophyllum lobbii*, *Bulbophyllum sumatranum* has elegant flowers that often exceed two to three inches.

Bulbophyllum fascinator, from the warmest regions in Vietnam and Laos, possesses flowers that range from six to eight inches in length, and is easily recognizable by its sepals, which are embellished with a fringe-like trim.

Bulbophyllum fascinator

Christensonia vietnamica

This species, discovered in 1989 in southern Vietnam, lives as an epiphyte in semi-deciduous, humid forests situated near streams at altitudes of approximately 350 feet. It is the only representative of its genus, *Christensonia*, a neighbor of the *Vanda* genus, and is monopodial and compact, with a stem that reaches a maximum length of twelve inches and has tough, short leaves. The flowers, one and a half inches wide, are large in proportion to the size of the plant.

Cymbidium ensifolium

This celebrated genus includes 52 species, principally terrestrial, that are distributed throughout Asia. In the Himalayas and China, these species are known for their large flowers and imposing bearing, and have frequently been used to create hybrids sold as potted plants and cut flowers.

Cymbidium ensifolium has the widest geographical distribution in its genus, and is an important inspiration in pictorial Chinese and Japanese art, due to its long, ribbon-like leaves and elegant, aromatic flowers. *Cymbidium devonianum*, a species native to Nepal, northeast India, and Thailand, has a compact bearing and hanging stems garnished with numerous crimson flowers, each approximately one and a half inches wide.

Cymbidium devonianum

Cypripedium calceolus

Cypripedium calceolus is a terrestrial species present in Eurasia, from France to Siberia, as well as in northeastern China. Long ago, it was relatively abundant in mountainous, calcareous regions, but today it has disappeared from many western European countries, making it a predominantly Asian flower.

Other species of Cypripedium live in North and Central America, as well as in temperate Asia. Thus, Cypripedium japonicum, which grows in bamboo forests in the mountains of Japan, Korea, and parts of China, produces a unique, large flower each spring. This flower is about four inches long, and is carried by a flowering stem that emerges from between two pleated leaves.

Cypripedium japonicum

Coelogyne pandurata

The 182 species of *Coelogyne* are sympodial orchids that most often boast white or ochre flowers, with a brown or yellow labellum. Though many types of *Coelogyne* bloom prolifically in greenhouses, *Coelogyne pandurata* is far to large to grow in such a confined setting. Stretching over three feet tall, its flowers are unusually marked with black and are nearly three feet in breadth, with pseudobulbs that are separated by a fairly long rhizome.

In contrast, *Coelogyne barbata* is a small plant that grows in India, Bhutan, Nepal, and on the slopes of the Himalayas, at altitudes of 3,000 to 6,000 feet. Its dark brown labellum is barbed, which led to its evocative name.

Coelogyne barbata

Dendrobium aduncum

Dendrobium is the second largest genus in terms of number of species, after *Bulbophyllum*. With nearly 1,200 species distributed throughout all of tropical and subtropical Asia, Australia, and the islands of the Pacific and New Zealand, the diversity among this genus is overwhelming.

Dendrobium aduncum is mostly distributed in southeast Asia. Like many *Dendrobium*, it has long, hanging, cane-like stems that lose their leaves in the dry season. Tight little knots of pink, vanilla-scented flowers form on the naked stems. *Dendrobium cruentum*, a species rare both in cultivation and nature, is fairly small and grows as an epiphyte in Thailand, at low altitudes. Its long-lasting flowers measure one and a half to two inches and are marked by a vibrant labellum streaked with red. Its pseudobulbs and leaves are covered with fine black hairs.

Dendrobium cruentum

Esmeralda clarkei

Esmeralda clarkei, similar in appearance to *Vanda*, is also known as *Arachnanthe clarkei*. This gorgeous species, rarely cultivated and thus highly prized, grows in the shade of the humid valleys east of the Himalayas. Its long monopodial stem is semi-hanging.

Holcoglossum kimballianum

Holcoglossum is a genus close to *Vanda*, though it possesses semi-cylindrical, rigid leaves. *Holcoglossum kimballianum*, a species that thrives in southern China, Thailand, and Burma, grows in big colonies on naked rocks, in full sun and at high altitudes. Its thick leaves help the flower survive nights where the temperatures plummet to 32°F. In cultivation, this species requires a cool resting period and good light in order to bloom fully.

Neofinetia falcata

This miniature plant has charming white flowers, which are aromatic and occasionally tinted pink. It has been cultivated for more than two centuries in Japan, where it is called *Fu Ran*. Historically, it was reserved for the samurai class, due to its status as a symbol of prosperity and nobility. Today, it continues to grow in Japan, as well as in Korea and the Ryukyu Islands, as an epiphyte on trees with deciduous foliage.

Paphiopedilum fairrieanum

Phalaenopsis bellina

Known as the 'moth orchid,' *Phalaenopsis* is a favorite for cultivation, as it blooms often and thrives under fairly simple conditions. So many hybrids are now available, that it easy to forget how few botanical species are at the root of this pervasive flower.

Phalaenopsis bellina is known for its beautiful blooms and heady perfume. *Phalaenopsis hieroglypica*, found only in the Phillipines, gets its name from the many hieroglyphic markings that dot its petals.

Phalaenopsis hieroglyphica

Renanthera auyongii

Certain species within this genus are extraordinarily tall, such as *Renanthera imschootiana*, whose vine-like stem climbs up sunny branches that can stretch more than sixteen feet long. The large, flowering stem forms at the top of the plant, and can carry approximately fifty luminous, red flowers, each two inches in breadth.

Lacking the drama of these giants, some species, like *Renanthera monachica* or *Renanthera bella*, are only five to eight feet tall, though they also possess beautiful red or orange flowers.

Renanthera imschootiana

Rhynchostylis gigantea

Rhynchostylis is a small genus, containing only four species: *Rhynchostylis retusa* and *Rhynchostylis praemorsa*, known for their white and pink flowers; *Rhynchostylis coelestis* with its rare sky-blue flowers; and *Rhynchostylis gigantean*, which, when in bloom, exhales a perfume so strong that it is almost unpleasant. *Rhyncostylis gigantean* has varied flowers, which can either be pure white or blood-red, or white with pink spots. These flowers are nicknamed "foxtail orchids" because of their pendulous stems, which are covered with tight clusters of blossoms.

Stereochilus dalatensis

This miniature orchid grows as an epiphyte in Vietnam, and has a 'hook' at the end of its column or gynostemium, which makes it easily recognizable from other miniature orchids. Its stem is covered with small pink flowers, each less than half an inch long.

In cultivation, these miniature orchids bloom spectacularly. They often have blooms that are larger than the plant, which makes them a nice addition to home or greenhouse collections.

Vanda tessellata

Vanda and its numerous hybrids are elegant, monopodial plants, whose generous flowering stems grow vivid flowers in a variety of colors. The celebrated *Vanda coerulea*, now very rare in nature, is one of the only orchids whose flowers are truly blue.

Vanda tessellata has large aromatic flowers, each with a labellum that is usually violet (though occasionally blue) and lightly checkered petals. This species can bloom all year long, particularly in its original regions in India, Burma, Nepal, Malaysia, and Sri Lanka. *Vanda liouvillei* has flowers that possess a unique, three-lobed labellum, with a center lobe that is divided at the end into two lobes of its own. It is known also for the weak development of its short stems.

Vanda liouvillei

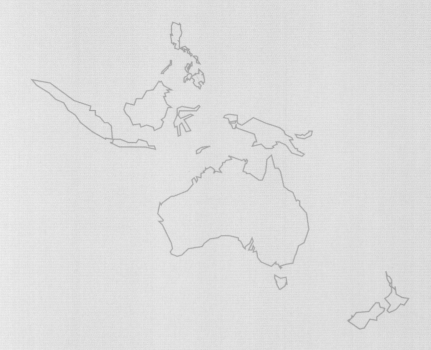

Oceania

Like Asia, Oceania's diverse climates foster a wide variety of orchids. The mountains of Papua New Guinea reach altitudes of nearly 15,000 feet and are filled with vibrant *Dendrobium*. In Australia, the vast desert regions have few orchids, though the humid zones in the north and northeast possess a very rich flora that includes numerous *Dendrobium* and *Bulbophyllum*, along with unique genera like *Dockrilla* and *Sarcochilus*. Certain regions have a lengthy dry season that alternates with a fairly short rainy season, creating a paradise for exceptionally beautiful terrestrial orchids, such as *Thelymitra*, which has striking blue flowers, *Pterostylis*, and *Diuris*.

Fog forest in the mountains of New Guinea

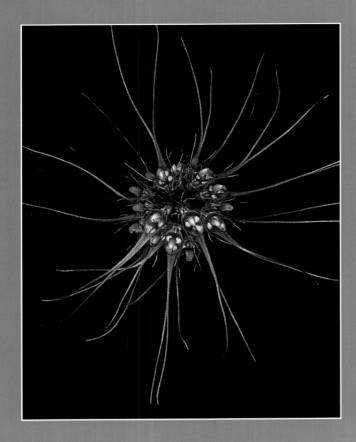

Bulbophyllum gracillimum

Some species of *Bulbophyllum* have flowering stems with a condensed, crown-like cluster of flowers. They make up the section of *Cirrhopetaloïdes* that includes *Bulbophyllum gracillimum*, which lives as an epiphyte on tree trunks in rainy forests, at low altitudes, in Australian Queensland, the Solomon Islands, new Caledonia, New Guinea, and also in Malaysia and Thailand. Each flower is approximately one inch in length and has two delicate lower sepals, which add to the flower's air of grace.

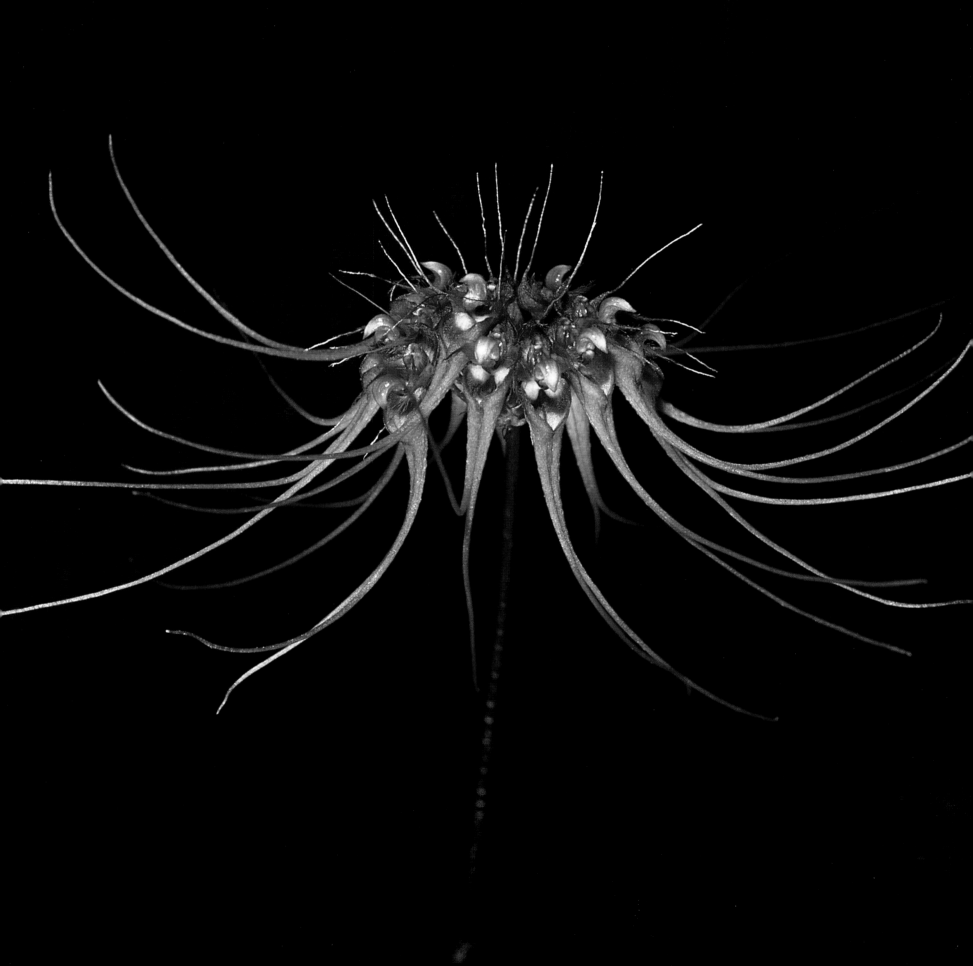

Dendrobium discolor

Dendrobium discolor forms large tufts of cane-like stems that are sixteen feet high and just over two inches wide. It grows in the northeast of Queensland and in New Guinea, and is covered with clusters of flowers that can reach three inches in breadth.

Dendrobium spectabile, which grows in New Guinea, the Solomon Islands, and Bougainvillea, has robust pseudobulbs that are two feet in length. Its clusters of brown-marked blooms are large, curvaceous, and grotesquely beautiful. Like *Dendrobium discolor*, these flowers are long-living, and last at least three months.

Dendrobium spectabile

Dockrillia linguiformis

Narrowly related to *Dendrobium*, the *Dockrillia* genus encompasses several Australian species whose climbing stems are garnished with thick, gnarled leaves. These leaves are actually water reserves, which have adapted to the strong sun that is part of the natural environment of the species.

Dockrillia linguiformis originates from Queensland and New South Wales, where it sometimes grows on exposed rocks, in climates marked by a dry season. Along with *Dockrillia wassellii*, it possesses white, crystalline flowers, that are less than an inch wide.

Dockrillia wassellii

Luisia teretifolia

This genus was named by the French botanist Gaudichaud-Beaupré in honor of Don Luis de Torrest, a nineteenth-century Spanish botanist. The species name refers to the shape of the plant's tapering leaves. *Luisia teretifolia* is distributed not only in Australia, where it grows primarily in the mangroves of Queensland, but also in New Guinea, Indonesia, and Malaysia. The small flowers (less than half an inch), appear regularly throughout the year, and stick to the stem in sets of two or three.

Phalaenopsis amabilis

Phalaenopsis amabilis is present primarily in New Guinea and Australia, but also in Java, Borneo, Ambon Island, and Sulawesi. It develops on low branches, on the fringes of forests, and requires a hot and humid climate. Along with two other species, *Phalaenopsis aphrodite* and *Phalaenopsis philippinensis*, it is the point of origin of many white-flowered hybrids.

In nature, these epiphyte plants have a pendulous bearing: rainwater flows along the leaves without ever stagnating in the heart formed by the youngest leaf. Thus, when cultivated in a pot, it is important to never leave water in the heart of the young plant, as it will lead to rot.

Index

Cover photograph: Comparettia macroplectron

All photography by Manuel Aubron, except
page 64: © Philippart de Foy/Explorer,
page 42: © Juan Carlos Muñoz AGE/Hoa-qui

Editor: Nichole Morford; Art Director: Dirk Kaufman; Managing Art Editor: Michelle Baxter; Executive Managing Editor: Sharon Lucas;
Publishing Director: Carl Raymond; DTP Coordinator: Kathy Farias; Production Manager: Ivor Parker

English translator: Nathalie Jordi
English translation © Dorling Kindersley, Ltd.

First American Edition, 2007
05 06 07 08 09 10 9 8 7 6 5 4 3 2 1

Published in the United States by DK Publishing/Dorling Kindersley, Ltd.
375 Hudson Street, New York, New York 10014

Originally published in the French by Hachette Pratique, under the title: Orchidées.
All text by Pascal Descourvierès
© 2005 HACHETTE LIVRE (Hachette Pratique), Paris

ISBN: 978-0-7566-2886-4
Printed in Malaysia by Tien Wah Press
Discover more at www.dk.com